Army
546,057 active

Air Force
328,812 active

U.S. Military
1,388,028 active

420,060 reserve

U.S. MILITARY
by the Numbers

Navy
314,339 active

Marine Corps
198,820 active

Branches

united
front

by Lisa M. Bolt Simons

Amie Jane Leavitt

Table

of Contents

To **Protect** and **Defend**

The United States military is a feared fighting force throughout the world. Brave men and women vow to defend the United States from all enemies, foreign and domestic. Prepare to view the military from an entirely new perspective. Let's break it down by the numbers.

1,082,777

The largest amount of active duty personnel stationed overseas; this occurred in 1968 during the Vietnam War (1959–1975).

31

Number of U.S. presidents who served in the military

Dwight D. Eisenhower

737

Number of overseas U.S. military installments

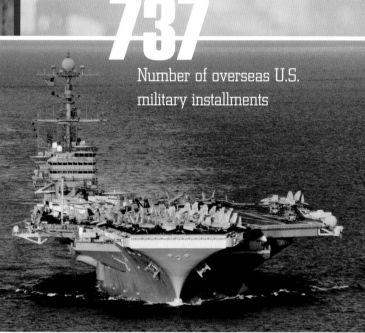

1,388,028

Number of total active duty military members as of September 30th, 2012

U.S. MARINES

Who does the United States government call in an emergency? The Marines! The United States Marine Corps, a branch of the United States Navy, is a rapid-reaction force.

First to Fight

In conflicts, a Marine Expeditionary Unit (MEU) is often the first force on the ground. An MEU can be called to action at any moment. An MEU includes 2,200 ground and air combat troops, their commanders, and the logistics crews that provide communications, vehicles, and supplies.

An MEU can go from first alert to action in just 6 hours.

hour 1 | Marine commanders receive orders.

hour 2 | Marine commanders and staff develop an action plan.

hour 3 | Marine ground, aviation, and logistics crews get ready to help with the mission.

hour 4 | Commander approves the plan and sends out orders for each Marine.

hour 5 | Marines prepare to move out, loading their gear onto vehicles.

hour 6 | The first wave of Marines is sent in.

	All Armed Services	Marines	Percentage of total that are Marines
Total Military Personnel	1,431,000	202,441	14%
Officers	234,000	21,307	9%
Enlisted	1,183,200	181,134	15%

*based on 2010 information

"Marines.
The Few, the Proud."

Marines by 7s

MEUs

ready to respond to
a crisis at any time

7

7 days

Sun.	Mon.	Tue.	Wed.	Thur.	Fri.	Sat.

a Marine's workweek

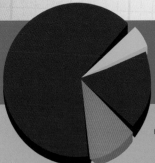

7.6%
enlisted Marines ages 31–35

7,331
spouses of Marines who
are also in the military

17.5%
enlisted Marines ages 26–30

7.9 lb.
weight of M27 Marine
Infantry Automatic Rifle

17 age of youngest enlisted Marines

DAY 77 days of constant attack that Marines endured in 1968 while defending the American base at Khe Sanh during the Vietnam War

70% percentage of Marines serving first enlistment

1775 year the Marines were founded

17,500 miles per hour speed that Marine Corps Colonel John Glenn traveled when he became the first American to orbit Earth in 1962

Careers in the Marines

Infantry: fighting force

32,749 Infantry Marine (all men)*

42 major job categories

293 specific roles

*In 2013 the Pentagon lifted its ban on women in combat roles.

Machine gunners **10%**

Reconnaissance men **2%**

Antitank Missilemen **7%**

Infantry Assaultmen **6%**

60% Infantrymen

15% Mortarmen

Aviation Ordnance:
Provide, maintain, and transport ordnance

2,831 Marines

2,651 Men

180 Women

Motor Transport:
Mechanics and vehicle operators

14,762 Marines
14,087 Men
675 Women

QUANTITY

M998	M936	M923	M105A2	M149A1
12	3	100	57	13

Military Police:
Military Police & Corrections

4,977 Marines

4,619 Men

358 Women

Marine Corps in the 20th Century

U.S. Involvement in World War I (1914–1918)

2 years of major U.S. engagements

9,520 Marines wounded in action

31,600 total Marines serving in war zone

2,461 Marines killed in battle

U.S. Involvement in World War II (1939–1945)

4 years, 8 months of major U.S. engagements

67,207 Marines wounded in action

485,883 Marines serving in war zone

19,733 Marines killed in battle

U.S. Involvement in the Korean War (1950—1953)

4 years of major U.S. engagements

about **130,000** total Marines serving in war zone

23,744 Marines wounded in action

4,268 Marines killed in battle

U.S. Involvement in the Vietnam War

(1959—1975)

Vietnam was the longest and bloodiest war in Marine history.

13,095 Marines killed in battle

88,594 Marines wounded in action

794,000 total Marines serving in war zone

7 years of major U.S. engagements

13

Iwo Jima

A Great Marine Victory

The Battle of Iwo Jima

Dates: February 19 to March 26, 1945
What: defining World War II battle
Where: Pacific Ocean south of Japan
Goal: capture island of Iwo Jima from Japanese Empire
Result: Japan surrendered the island to the Marines

2 number of U.S. flags Marines raised atop Mt. Suribachi

1st flag raised: 10:30 a.m.
2nd flag raised: 12 p.m.
The second flag was larger than the first and is the event famously captured by photographer Joe Rosenthal.

3 number of Marines pictured in Rosenthal's photo who died in the battle after the flag-raising

About **22,000** Japanese troops dug **11** miles of underground tunnels.

36 days of battle

700 ships transported Marines and cargo to Iwo Jima.

77,000 Marines from 3rd, 4th, and 5th Marine divisions took part in the battle.

Of the **22,000** Japanese soldiers, only about **1,100** survived.

More than **21,000** Marines were wounded.

Nearly **7,000** Marines died.

1/3 of all Marines killed in World War II died on Iwo Jima.

27 Medals of Honor were awarded, **13** posthumously.

Iwo Jima:

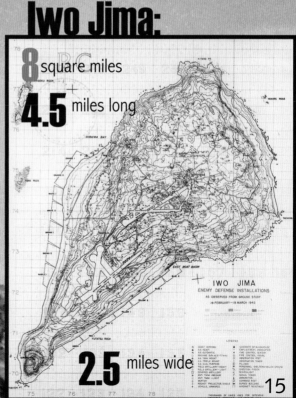

8 square miles

4.5 + miles long

2.5 miles wide

IWO JIMA
ENEMY DEFENSE INSTALLATIONS

15

Becoming a Marine

Basic Training

The physical requirements of basic training are different for men and women. In all other training, men and women must meet the same standards.

Processing
1 week
medical checkups,
physical fitness testing,
and getting supplies

Phase 1
4 weeks
physical conditioning;
self-defense; marching;
Marine Corps customs,
history, and values training;
weapons training; first aid training

Phase 2
4 weeks
water survival and
weapons marksmanship

Phase 3
4 weeks
basic warrior skills;
defensive driving
course; land navigation;
basic field skills

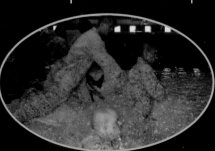

Activity

Hours Spent
in Basic Training

487: Eating

13: Marching

572: Sleeping

34.5: Drill practice

41: Academic studies

34: Ethics and values training

54: The Crucible (final testing)

5: On-base liberty on Family Day

60: Senior drill instructor time

106: Free time (includes 4-5 hours on Sundays & holidays)

146: Daily routine (showering, grooming, caring for clothing and room)

81: Physical training/conditioning

225.5: Instruction time (combat, water survival, weapons, field training)

Contents of a Marine Recruit's Seabag

1
- reflective safety belt
- desert cap
- woodland cap
- field desert
  boonie cap
- green sweatshirt
- pair green
  sweatpants
- pair combat boots
- pair jungle boots
- pair shower shoes
- pair running shoes
- pair book bands
- hygiene kit
- sewing kit
- green towel
- green washcloth
- flashlight
- jock strap
- mouthpiece
- boot brush
- pair of gloves
- poncho
- cartridge belt
- canteen cup
- Gore-Tex® top
- pillow
- plastic pillowcase
- fabric pillowcase
- mattress cover

2
- duffel bags
- khaki belts with
  gold-plated tips
- pairs of woodland trousers
- woodland blouses
- laundry bags
- 1-quart canteens
- canteen covers
- blankets
- sheets

3
- gym trunks
- pairs of
  desert trousers
- desert blouses
- pairs of white socks

6
- undershirts
- pairs of brown
  boot socks
- pairs of underwear

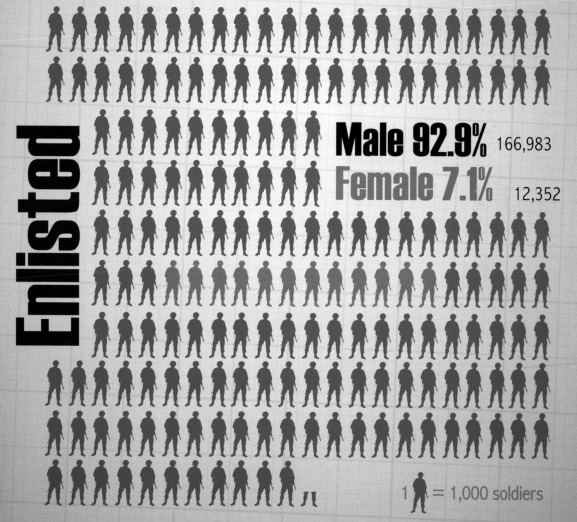

Officers

Male **93.8%** 20,498
Female **6.2%** 1,348

1 = 1,000 officers

Enlisted

Male **92.9%** 166,983
Female **7.1%** 12,352

1 = 1,000 soldiers

The Crucible:
A Rite of Passage

All Marines go through 12 weeks of intense training during boot camp. That training leads up to a final combat exercise called The Crucible.

29: number of problem-solving exercises performed

54: number of hours The Crucible lasts

48: number of miles marched

24: number of logs climbed over and under while carrying supplies

45: pounds of gear carried

36 stations

including exercises such as:

working as a team to overcome
obstacles in an exercise called 12 Stalls

crossing two horizontal
cable-supported logs

climbing 8-foot-high
horizontal log

crossing 52-foot-long
ropes carrying
ammunition cans and
water cans

climbing up and down a 10-foot
wall on a knotted rope

retrieving "wounded" dummy
from top of 18-foot tower

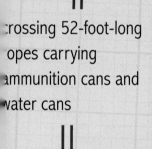

carrying supplies across two 52-foot-long
ropes suspended 2 feet and 10 feet off
the ground

Equipping the Marines

weapons

M16
service rifle
Ammunition: 5.56 x 45 mm rounds
Maximum Range: 3,600 meters
Rate of Fire: 12 to 15 rounds a minute

M203
grenade launcher
Ammunition: 40 mm grenades
Maximum Range: 350 meters
Rate of Fire: single-shot

M249 SAW
automatic weapon
Ammunition: 5.56 x 45 mm rounds
Maximum Range: 3,600 meters
Rate of Fire: 85 rounds a minute

M777 Howitzer

long-range cannon
Ammunition: 155 mm / 39-caliber rounds
Maximum Range: 30 kilometers
Rate of Fire: 5 rounds a minute

M9 Beretta

lightweight pistol
Ammunition: 9 mm rounds
Maximum Range: 50 meters
Rate of Fire: semiautomatic

FGM-148 Javelin

missile
Ammunition: missiles
Maximum Range: 2,500 meters
Rate of Fire: single-shot

Distance

	2,000 meters	16,000 meters	32,000 meters
M16	3,600 meters		
M203	350 meters		
M249 SAW	3,600 meters		
M777 Howitzer			30,000 meters
M9 Beretta	50 meters		
FGM-148 Javelin	2,500 meters		

M-ATV

all-terrain vehicle
Weight: 25,000 lb.
Size: 20.5 ft. long; 8.2 ft. wide

AAV-7

amphibious assault vehicle
Weight: 26 tons (fully loaded with a three-man crew)
Capacity: 21 combat-loaded Marines, 3 crew members, 10,000 lb. of cargo

LAV

armored fighting tank
Weight: 24,980 lb.
Crew: 3-man crew
Weapons: 2 grenade launchers, 25 mm cannon, two M240 machine guns

Vehicles

HMMWV

high mobility multipurpose
wheeled vehicle
Weight: 5,200 lb.
Special features: armored plating,
bullet-resistant glass

MTVR

crew and supply transport vehicle
Weight: 7 tons
Capacity: 20 tons

Top Speeds

AAV-7

LAV

M-ATV

HMMWV

45 mph

62.5 mph

65 mph

75 mph

The MV-22B Osprey

The MV-22B Osprey was first used in combat in 2007. It increased the Marines' ability to outmaneuver their enemies. The Osprey has the speed and range of an airplane, but it takes off and lands like a helicopter. It can carry 24 combat Marines from a ship to a land base. The Osprey can go twice as fast and five times farther than previous helicopters.

Weight

52,600 lb.

Cost per unit

$72-$95 million

Wingspan

84.6 ft.

Range

990 miles

Crew

3 ⎡ pilot
⎢ copilot
⎣ crew chief

Cruising Speed

322 miles per hour

Capacity

24 combat troops

13

Length

57 ft., **3** in.

Height

22 ft., **1** in.

Beyond the Battlefield

Marine Corps Disaster Relief

The Marine Corps seeks to make the world a safer, better place. Part of that mission involves providing emergency relief when natural disasters hit.

Earthquake in Haiti (January 2010)

The 24th Marine Expeditionary Unit delivered and distributed:

57,368 meals

1,365,617 lb. of rice

589,764 bottles of water

2,781 hand-crank radios

22,064 lb. of medical supplies

79,656 jars of baby food

more than **1,000,000** disaster relief rations

15,207 lb. of other supplies

Flooding in Pakistan
(August 2010)

2,200
Marines responded.

U.S. helicopters rescued **3,075** people.

Marines delivered
650,000
lb. of relief supplies.

Typhoon in the Philippines
(December 2010)

500 relief aid boxes

40 generators

165 tons
of relief supplies
delivered, including:

250 boxes of blankets

14,500 family ration packs

49,000 lb. of rice

833 sleeping mats

147 bundles of mosquito nets

29

Marine Special Operations

Marine Special Operations units are small teams trained to work with foreign armies, defeat terrorists, gather sensitive information, and complete other missions.

Marine Special Operations Command (MARSOC) was activated in 2006. The Marine Special Operations Regiments (MSOR) are combat units based on those used in a 2003 pilot program. In that program, a unit was composed of:

30-man reconnaissance team

29-man intelligence team

7-man combat team

1 headquarters team

Today 2,500 Marines are in Special Operations. Each highly trained unit is sent overseas as needed.

Marine Special Operations Training

Phase 1 10 weeks swimming, running, rucking, hand-to-hand combat, mission planning, fire support, land navigation, combat medic training

Phase 2 8 weeks

intelligence gathering, sea navigation,

small boat handling, field training in urban and non-urban environments

5 weeks **Phase 3**

close-quarters combat, marksmanship, shooting and moving as a team

7 weeks **Phase 4**

how to think like the enemy in order to stop acts of terror, guerilla warfare, or rebellion

U.S. AIR FORCE

The men and women of the United States Air Force
are prepared to protect their own country. They will
conduct any mission they are asked to perform.

Fast, Faster, Fastest

When Orville and Wilbur Wright built their first military plane in 1909, its speed was 42 miles per hour (mph). Today Air Force planes fly faster than the speed of sound.

F-100 Super Sabre
first aircraft able to fly faster than the speed of sound in level flight

- 1953: date operational
- 18,185 lb.: weight
- 38 ft., 10 in: wingspan
- 16,000 lb.: thrust
- 900 mph: top speed

Wright Military Flyer

- 1909: year operational
- 735 lb.: weight
- 36.5 ft.: wingspan
- 2 propellers
- 42 mph: top speed

SR-71 Blackbird
remains the highest and fastest flying manned aircraft of any nation on record

- 1964: date operational
- 140,000 lb.: weight fully loaded
- 55 ft., 7 in.: wingspan
- 65,000 lb.: thrust
- about 2,000 mph: top speed

F-22 Raptor

- 2005: date operational
- 43,340 lb.: weight
- 44 ft., 6 in.: wingspan
- 70,000 lb.: thrust
- 1,100 mph: top speed

- Mach 1 = the speed of sound, about 755 mph
- Mach 2 = two times the speed of sound
- Mach 3 = three times the speed of sound

The 1-2-3s of Becoming an Airman

0 hairs:
Barbers shave all male recruits' heads so there are 0 hairs left.

1 M16:
Each airman is issued an M16 rifle.

2 minutes:
maximum amount of time in which recruits must be able to assemble their M16s

3 events in the Basic Military Training Physical Fitness Test:
to be done in a 3-hour window with a minimum of 3 minutes between each event (one minute of push-ups, one minute of sit-ups, and a timed 1.5—mile run)

4:45 a.m.:
time recruits must wake up during basic training

5 week 5 of basic training:
Recruits switch from learning fighting skills on mannequins to using pugil sticks to face off against fellow recruits.

6 week 6:
Recruits go to Basic Expeditionary Airman Skills Training (BEAST), where they experience realistic combat situations.

7 items NOT allowed at basic training:
- personal running shoes
- radio/CD player/ MP3 player
- food
- magazines
- makeup
- expensive jewelry
- tobacco in any form

8 weeks of basic training

9:00 p.m.:
lights out

10 pull-ups:
one of several physical requirements a recruit must meet in order to earn the Warhawk, the highest honor at graduation

Weapons

Pilots in the Air Force are the best of the best. And when the time comes to fight, they are armed and ready with the best military planes and weapons.

A-10 Thunderbolt II

Various weapons carried:

- 1 GAU-8/A 7-barrel gun
- 4 AIM-9 Sidewinder missiles
- 6 AGM-65 Maverick missiles
- 6 2,000-lb. bombs
- 10 cluster bombs
- 18 500-lb. bombs
- 28 rockets

B-1B Lancer

Various weapons carried:

- 8 2,000-lb. mines
- 15 500-lb. bombs
- 48 2,000-lb. bombs
- 30 cluster bombs
- 84 500-lb. mines

B-52H Stratofortress

Various weapons carried:

- 8 nuclear warheads
- 79 mines
- 52 missiles
- 133 bombs

F-22 Raptor

Various weapons carried:

- 1 6-barrel cannon
  with 480 rounds
- 2 Sidewinder missiles
- 6-8 radar-guided missiles
- 2 bombs

LGM-30G Minuteman III

an intercontinental ballistic missile (ICBM);
fired from the ground

- 6,000-mile range
- 79,432 lb.
- 15,000 mph (Mach 23):
  speed missile travels

Today's Air Force

67,728 staff sergeants

26,437 master sergeants

5,047 senior master sergeants

2,631 chief master sergeants

81.2% men

18.8% women

332,918

total Air Force Active Duty

64,932 officers

80.8% men

19.2% women

263,964 enlisted

55,514 senior airmen

50,837 airmen 1st class

4,269 airmen

9,733 airmen basic (no insignia)

4,022 cadets

77.8% men

22.2% women

3,579 colonels

147 brigadier generals

99 major generals

44 lieutenant generals

14 generals

*numbers accurate as of September 30, 2013

Inventory of aircraft

805 transports

1,213 trainers

2,025 fighters and attackers

202 helicopters

162 bombers

507 tankers

126 special operations aircraft

511 intelligence, surveillance, and reconnaissance aircraft

86 bases worldwide

1 female four-star general in Air Force history, Janet Wolfenbarger, promoted in June 2012

6,907 second lieutenants

7,472 first lieutenants

22,157 captains

29 average age of enlisted airman

14,518 majors

9,995 lieutenant colonels

1 five-star general in Air Force history, Henry "Hap" Arnold, promoted in 1949

729 female pilots

Working the Sky and Space

The Air Force isn't just responsible for what's happening in the skies. Trained airmen use the latest technology to monitor space.

20,000 objects in space, including satellites, that airmen in the Air Force Space Command track

50,000 miles of space that airmen track

4 sources of photographs and videos from space (satellites, aircraft, remotely piloted aircraft [RPA], and airmen)

30,000 feet: top altitude at which the Critical Care Air Transport Team (CCATT) can function. This team is able to treat any number of medical issues that may arise while airmen are in flight.

+3 members in the CCATT (a critical care physician, a critical care

4

special operations forces
in the Air Force:

- Combat Controllers (CCT)—direct air traffic
  in remote, and often hostile, areas

- Pararescuemen (PJ)—parachute into dangerous
  conditions to recover personnel and provide medical aid

- Tactical Air Control Party (TACP)—plan, order,
  and communicate about weapon strikes

- Special Operations Weather Technicians
  (SOWT)—keep close track of weather conditions
  where special operations units are deployed

40+

pounds of radio and
marking equipment TACP
specialists carry

24

hours a day
a PJ must be on alert
to go save a life

3

conditions in which an SOWT must
be able to collect data, analyze it, and
make predictions (oceanographic,
meteorological, and space atmosphere)

The Air Force in 3s

30 seconds:
time it takes an experienced airman to disassemble and assemble an M16 training rifle

3 core values:
(integrity, service before self, excellence in all we do)

35 average age of Air Force officers

3 active duty personnel in 1907

13th of October 1942

The Tuskegee Airmen, the first African-American fighter group in the Army Air Force (AAF), is activated.

*The Army Air Force became the United States Air Force in 1947.

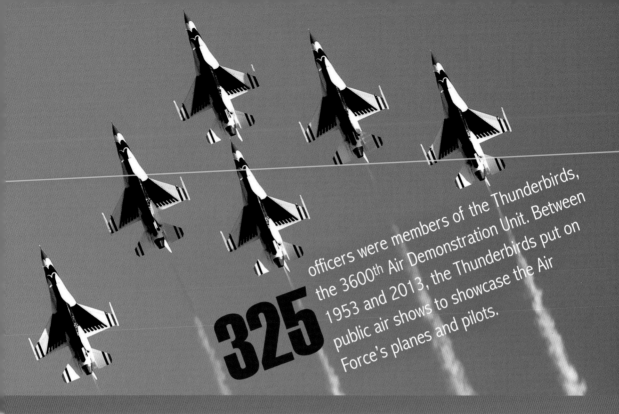

325 officers were members of the Thunderbirds, the 3600th Air Demonstration Unit. Between 1953 and 2013, the Thunderbirds put on public air shows to showcase the Air Force's planes and pilots.

$30,000 amount the U.S. Army paid the Wright brothers for their Wright Military Flyer in 1909

Bombers of
World War II:
The United States vs. Germany

After World War I (1914–1918), the AAF realized it needed a bomber that could travel long distances from a base, loaded with weapons. At the same time, the bomber needed to be able to defend itself from an attack. The B-17 was the first to do both. The Germans also had their share of bombers, such as the Junkers Ju 88s, but the AAF's fleet was better.

B-17 Flying Fortress

3,750
miles: maximum range

1935 year the prototype (Model 299) made its first flight

13 model 299s ordered

640,000 tons of bombs dropped during World War II

12,726 total B-17 models made when production ended in 1945

9,600 lb.: weight of bombs carried

287 mph: top speed

62 enemy fighters shot down by the 390th Bombardment Group, the highest kill rate in a single day (October 10, 1943) for any bomber or fighter group

Junkers Ju 88 (German bomber)

1936 year the prototype first flew

nearly **15,000** total Junker Ju 88 models made when production ended in 1945

300 planes first ordered by Nazi leader Adolf Hitler

6,600 lb.: weight of bombs carried

292 mph: top speed

1,696 miles: range

around **40,000** people killed when Germany bombed London and other European cities between September 1940 and May 1941

Fighters and Aces
in World War II

World War II (1939–1945) fighter pilots faced battle in the skies in cramped, single-seat aircraft. The U.S. pilots who shot down five or more enemies were called "aces."

Lieutenant Boyd "Buzz" Wagner

1st ace of the war (1941)
8 enemy fighters shot down

Major Richard Bong

was called the "Ace of Aces"
40 enemy fighters shot down
200 combat missions
500 combat hours
1 Medal of Honor

Major Thomas McGuire Jr.

38 enemy fighters shot down
1 Medal of Honor

Lockheed P-38 Lightning

7 of the 8 top aces flew this fighter
4 machine guns
1 cannon

414 mph: top speed
1,300 miles: range
40,000 ft.: maximum altitude

North American P-51D Mustang

6 machine guns
2,000 lb.: weight of bombs carried
437 mph: top speed
1,000 miles: range
41,900 ft.: maximum altitude

Republic P-47 Thunderbolt

6-8 machine guns
2,500 lb.: weight of
bombs carried
433 mph: top speed
1,030 miles: range
42,000 ft.: maximum altitude

The "Torture Chamber"

The McKinley Climatic Laboratory at Eglin Air Force Base in Florida is often called the torture chamber. Every type of Air Force aircraft and equipment is tested in this laboratory in simulated extreme-weather environments. Even guns and missiles can be fired within the chambers.

55,775 square ft.: area inside the Main Chamber (MC)

6 chambers

117 square ft.: area inside the smallest chamber, the Temperature-Altitude (TA) Chamber

82,000 ft.: maximum altitude simulated in the TA chamber

7 stories tall at the center of the MC

2 main front doors, each weighing 200 tons, which slide apart to get aircraft in and out of the MC

15 minutes: time it takes for the main front doors to slide open or to close

-104°F lowest recorded temperature in the Equipment Test Chamber

225°F highest recorded temperature in the TA Chamber

560 mph: highest wind speed tested on a small area of an aircraft

75 mph: highest wind speed tested on an entire aircraft

$150,000 average monthly electric bill for the laboratory

16 simulated weather situations

$15,000 cost per day at which a private company can rent the MC to test its own non-military equipment

Becoming a Pilot

As part of their intense training, pilots must get used to strong forces that the body feels as it changes speed over time. These forces are measured in Gs. One G is the same as the force of gravity. A person with no training can withstand 5 times the force of gravity, or 5 Gs, in an aircraft before passing out. Passing out for this reason is called gravity loss of consciousness (GLOC). With a special G suit and training, that number rises to 9. Aircraft controls prevent Gs much greater than 9 in order to keep pilots safe.

Physical Requirements to be an Air Force Pilot:

20/30 minimum for near vision: each eye must be correctable to 20/20

20/70 minimum for distant vision: each eye must be correctable to 20/20

64-77 inches: standing height

34-40 inches: sitting height

12 years old: no hay fever, asthma, or allergies after this age

1,000

approximate number of new Air Force pilots certified each year

At 9 Gs, a body weighing 175 lb. feels like 1,575 lb.

At 5 Gs, a body weighing 175 lb. feels like 875 lb.

5.9 G forces: felt on Shock Wave, a roller coaster at Six Flags Over Texas

4.1 G forces: felt with a slap on the back

2.9 G forces: felt in the average sneeze

1 G force: Humans typically experience this every day, which is normal gravity at sea level.

120 days:

first phase of training

- 213 hours: classroom time
- 30 days: preflight ground training
- 48 hours: time in flight simulator
- 87 hours: time in actual flight

120 days:

advanced phase of training
3 choices:

1. Fighter / Bomber Track (T-38C Talon)
- 178 hours: classroom time
- 38 hours: simulator time
- 96 hours: flight time

2. Airlift / Tanker Track (T-1A Jayhawk)
- 143 hours: classroom time
- 54 hours: simulator time
- 76 hours: flight time

3. Rotary-Wing Helicopter Track (TH-1H Huey)
- 130 hours: classroom time
- 40 hours: simulator time
- 105 hours: flight time

Operation Enduring Freedom

September 11, 2001
Terrorists attack the United States.

19 members of the Afghanistan-based terrorist group al-Qaida hijacked U.S. passenger planes.

4 airplanes were taken over by the hijackers.

About **3,000** people were killed when hijacked planes crashed into the Pentagon in Washington, D.C., the World Trade Center towers in New York City, and a field in Pennsylvania.

October 7, 2001 – December 18, 2011

March 2–16, 2002

Operation Enduring Freedom

Operation ANACONDA

As a result of the terrorist attacks, the United States launched Operation Enduring Freedom (2001–present). U.S. military forces began to fight against al-Qaida and the Taliban.

31 targets were hit by B-1 and B-52 bombers.

Nearly **70** percent of the bombs the United States used were precision guided.

More than **2,000** U.S. military members died.

More than **18,000** U.S. military members were wounded.

U.S. military forces and their allies attempted to destroy al-Qaida and Taliban forces.

10,000 ft.: height of the mountains where the Taliban and al-Qaida set up their defense

751 bombs dropped in the first 48 hours to support ground troops

667 bombs dropped on March 9 and 10

8 U.S. service members killed

82 U.S. service members wounded

The Air Force in 7s

7 crew members on a C-5 Galaxy, the largest aircraft in the Air Force inventory, with a maximum cargo capacity of 270,000 pounds

17 the youngest a person can be to join the Air Force

17 obstacles in the course at Basic Military Training

700 rounds per minute shot from an M4 carbine with an M203 grenade launcher

more than **7,000** miles: the range of Air Force One, the president's plane

70,000 ft.: cruising altitude of the high-flying manned reconnaissance U-2 aircraft

$70 million budget of the Air Force Academy for cadet pay and allowances in 2014

$759 million budget for ammunition in 2014

Unmanned Aerial Vehicles

In the early 1960s, Air Force unmanned aerial vehicles (UAVs) flew for the National Reconnaissance Office. This organization was so secret that the name was classified until 1992. In the Vietnam War, UAVs were used to assess bomb damage. By 1999 Predator UAVs were providing commanders with enemy target information. After September 11, 2001, the unmanned vehicles were used more often.

X-51A WaveRider

(experimental)

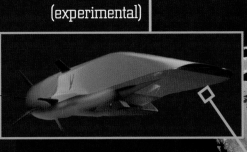

Time an X-51A WaveRider can travel from Las Vegas to various points in the world

X-51A WaveRider

The X-51A WaveRider offers the Air Force a promising future for hypersonic flight—that is five times the speed of sound!

2010: year operational
25 ft.: length
4,000 lb.: weight
270 lb.: fuel capacity
3,600+ mph: top speed
70,000+ ft.: altitude

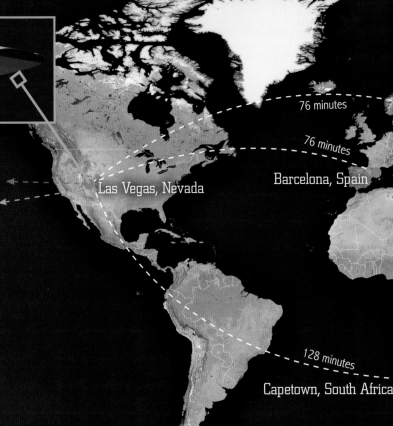

76 minutes

76 minutes

Barcelona, Spain

Las Vegas, Nevada

128 minutes

Capetown, South Africa

MQ-1B Predator

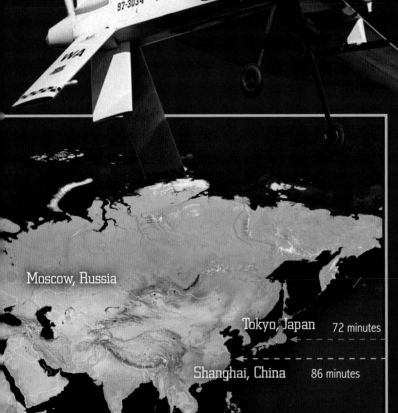

97-3034

WA

Moscow, Russia

Tokyo, Japan   72 minutes

Shanghai, China   86 minutes

MQ-1B Predator

The MQ-1B Predator has been widely used in recent years to collect intelligence about enemies and make strikes.

2005: year operational
4-cylinder engine
115 horsepower
55 ft.: wingspan
1,130 lb.: weight empty
665 lb.: fuel capacity
84 to 135 mph: speed
25,000 ft.: maximum altitude
2 laser-guided AGM-114 Hellfire missiles
2 remote crew members on the ground, a pilot and a sensor operator
$20 million: cost for one MQ-1B Predator system as of 2009

U.S. ARMY

For more than 200 years, soldiers in the United States
Army have protected their nation. Soldiers train their bodies
and minds to perform well, even in life-threatening conditions.
From weaponry to what a recruit needs for basic training, this
is the Army——by the numbers.

America's Soldiers

The Soldiers

All Army soldiers are expected to embody 7 core values: loyalty, duty, respect, selfless service, honor, integrity, and personal courage.

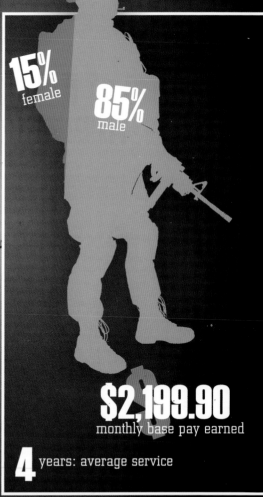

15% female

85% male

$2,199.90
monthly base pay earned

4 years: average service

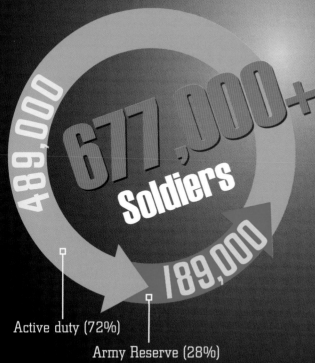

489,000

677,000+

Soldiers

189,000

Active duty (72%)

Army Reserve (28%)

officers (17%)   enlisted (83%)

59

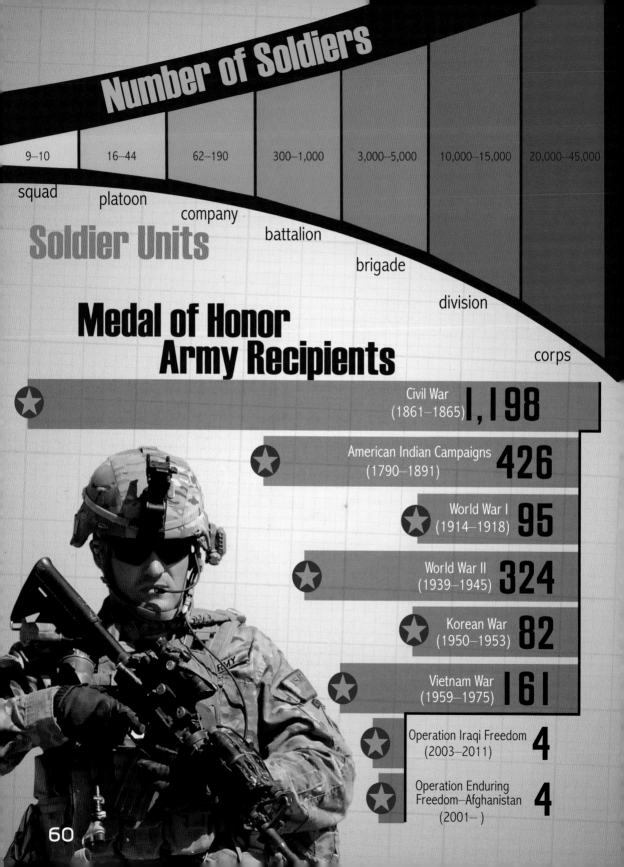

Number of Soldiers

| 9–10 | 16–44 | 62–190 | 300–1,000 | 3,000–5,000 | 10,000–15,000 | 20,000–45,000 |

Soldier Units

squad
platoon
company
battalion
brigade
division
corps

Medal of Honor
Army Recipients

Civil War
(1861–1865) **1,198**

American Indian Campaigns
(1790–1891) **426**

World War I
(1914–1918) **95**

World War II
(1939–1945) **324**

Korean War
(1950–1953) **82**

Vietnam War
(1959–1975) **161**

Operation Iraqi Freedom
(2003–2011) **4**

Operation Enduring
Freedom–Afghanistan
(2001–) **4**

The Army in 3s

3 phases in the Army's Basic Combat Training (BCT): Red, White, and Blue

13 Army job code number for anything to do with Field Artillery; specific numbers and letters are assigned to each Military Occupational Specialty (MOS).

30 number of soldiers in a platoon that carries 400 pounds of batteries to power equipment during a 3-day mission

33 number of combat-equipped soldiers that can be carried in a Boeing CH-47 Chinook, the Army's largest helicopter

103 number of years after his time in combat President Theodore Roosevelt was awarded the Medal of Honor

3,000+ rounds in a 7.62 mm machine gun on a Stryker MGS vehicle

362,015 number of soldiers serving in the Army National Guard in 2010

$30,000 maximum bonus for a 3-year enlistment

61

Army Weapons

WEAPON		WEIGHT
M9 pistol		(loaded) **2.6 lb.**
M24A3 sniper rifle		(loaded) **18.3 lb.**
MK19-3 40 mm Grenade Machine Gun		**72.4 lb.**
M224 Mortar (conventional)		**48 lb.**
M120/M121 Mortar		**319 lb.**
M109A6 Paladin		(combat ready) **63,615 lb.**

AMMO	RANGE
15 rounds	**50 meters**
5 rounds	**1.2 km**
up to **375 rounds** per minute	**2.2 km**
18-30 rounds per minute for 1-4 minutes	**3.5 km**
16 rounds for first minute, then 4 rounds per minute	**7.2 km**
4 rounds per minute for first 3 minutes, then 1 round per minute	**30 km**

The Abrams Tank

No vehicle is more identified with the United States Army than the Abrams tank. This tank provides soldiers with mobility, protection, and firepower.

1980 entered United States service

Top Speed
41.5 miles per hour

Width
12 feet

Height
8 feet

Length
32 feet

Weapons on M1A1

120 mm XM256 smooth bore cannon

.50-caliber M2 machine gun

Ammunition Storage

- 42 rounds—120 mm gun
- 11,400 rounds—7.62 mm gun
- 900 rounds—.500-caliber gun
- 32 screening grenades

Weight
67.6 tons

A Ready Soldier

$5,000+
the average value of equipment and clothing for each soldier

Soldiers are issued their general gear at BCT. Once they arrive at their post, they must check in at the Central Issue Facility (CIF). This is where they receive gear and clothing that is specific to their unit or geographic location. Depending on the weather at the post and the type of mission, some of what is issued varies. Ammunition, chemical protection, and other gear is provided later and varies according to the mission.

1 advanced combat helmet (ACH)

1 ATN PVS7-2 Night Vision Goggles (NVGs)

1 Ghillie Suit—camouflage that has artificial vegetation on it for better concealment

1 M16 rifle

2 first-aid kits

4 uniforms

2 Army Combat Uniforms (ACU) with camouflage pattern

2 ACUs with fire resistance

1 set of body armor

1 vest

4 protective and ballistic inserts

8 tan T-shirts

1 M40 series gas mask

4 choices of water container; all have a tube that can be used with a gas mask

4 pairs of underwear (male soldiers)

0 undergarments (female soldiers–self-equipped)

1 Joint Service Lightweight Integrated Suit Technology (JSLIST) for chemical protection

Battle of the Bulge, World War II

The Battle of the Bulge is considered one of the largest and bloodiest battles of World War II. German dictator Adolf Hitler wanted to break apart the American and British forces stationed in Europe. In the winter of 1944, he ordered a surprise attack in the forests of northwest Europe. The German soldiers pushed through the Allied forces and formed a bulge in the Allied lines. But the Allies fought back and eventually pushed the Germans back. The U.S. Army was a major force in the victory.

16 December 16, 1944: the day the Germans attacked

3 weeks: time the battle lasted

75 mile stretch of the Ardennes Forest, dense woods with few roads where four American divisions were resting

about

600,000

American soldiers fighting

1 word spoken when the acting commander of the U.S. 101st Airborne Division was told to surrender. He said, "Nuts!" and refused.

500 pounds: weight of the bomb that killed 30 wounded U.S. soldiers along with nurse Renee Lemaire on December 24, 1944, at an American Aid Station

about

200,000

German troops

80,000

approximate number of American soldiers killed, wounded, or captured

100,000

approximate number of Germans killed, wounded, or captured

3 times U.S. General Omar Bradley had to prove his identity. He did this by answering questions about American football and actress Betty Grable. U.S. soldiers were forced to prove their identities after some English-speaking Germans had impersonated U.S. soldiers.

69

Then and Now

1949

Soldier's average monthly pay:

enlisted Private/less than
4 months of service:

$75

Colonel/less than
2 years of service:

$570

General/less than
2 years of service:

$926

new house: **$7,450**

new car: **$1,420**

gallon of gas: **$0.17**

2013

Soldier's average monthly pay:

enlisted Private/less than
4 months of service:

$1,402

Colonel/less than
2 years of service:

$6,064

General/less than
2 years of service:

$14,975

new house: **$200,000**

new car: **$30,000**

gallon of gas: **$3.38**

Operation Iraqi Freedom

On March 17, 2003, President George W. Bush demanded that Iraqi dictator Saddam Hussein and his sons leave Iraq within 48 hours. They had committed criminal acts against Iraqis and neighboring countries. President Bush also believed Hussein had weapons of mass destruction. Hussein didn't leave the country. The U.S. invasion of Iraq began on March 20, 2003. The six-week invasion turned into an eight-and-a-half-year war that officially ended in 2011.

170,000+ U.S. troops stationed in Iraq at more than 500 bases at the peak of the war

1,500,000+ Americans served in Iraq

6,000,000+ miles an Army transportation battalion recorded during about 300 convoys, supplying 20 bases in Iraq

32,226 Americans wounded

4,487 Americans died

nearly **9,000** awards given to soldiers for bravery

$1.7 trillion cost of the Iraq war and war-related expenses

March 23, 2003

32

U.S. Army Apache helicopters searched for 40,000 Iraqi Republican Guard troops hidden south of Baghdad.

April 9, 2003

39 feet

height of the Saddam Hussein statue that was pulled down by Iraqi men and U.S. troops

December 13, 2003

2:30 a.m.

time when the last U.S. troops started to secretly leave Iraq

8 feet

depth of the hole in which Saddam Hussein was hiding when he was captured by U.S. troops

December 18, 2011

73

Working in the Army

The Army has more than 150 jobs to choose from, from fighting on the front lines to playing in a military band. Special tests help identify career options for recruits.

- detects mines
- basic demolition
- builds bridges
- makes obstacles

14 WEEKS OF TRAINING

Combat Engineer

main combat forces on the ground; may lead to advanced training such as sniper or airborne school

14 WEEKS OF TRAINING

Infantry

5 FUNCTIONS

1. support operations
2. site security
3. law and order
4. military prisoners
5. intelligence

Military Police

47 specialties from allergies to heart surgery

provides health care to soldiers and their families

Medical Corps

1 language other than English that recruits learn to understand fluently

1 qualification for top secret clearance needed to go to training

27 CAREER OPTIONS

20 WEEKS OF ADVANCED TRAINING

keeps vehicles and machines working, from medical equipment to missile systems

Human Intelligence Collector

Mechanic

D-Day

"D-Day" refers to the first day of the Normandy Invasion during World War II. This two-month-long battle began to free western Europe from the grip of Nazi Germany. It was a turning point in the war, and the U.S. Army played a major role.

June 6, 1944
invasion

160,000
Allied troops landed along the beaches

55 number of divisions of soldiers the Germans had in France

133,000+ soldiers began the march across Europe to defeat the Germans

12 Medal of Honor recipients

19 U.S. Army divisions

5 beach code names
Utah
Omaha
Gold
Juno
Sword

By June 30, 1944, the following had landed on the Normandy shores:

850,000+ men

148,000 vehicles

570,000 tons of supplies

4,000 to 9,000 German soldiers killed or wounded

50 number of miles of Normandy coastline where the Allied troops landed

13,000+ Allied parachute troopers jumped behind enemy lines five hours before the attack on the beach.

10,300+ Allied soldiers killed or wounded

K-9s

Dogs serve alongside human soldiers in the U.S. Army. The K-9 Corps provides protection and support in peacetime and during battles.

March 1942

The K-9 Corps was established.

18,000 dogs went to training centers when program began

8,000 dogs failed initial exams

8 weeks training, minimum; 12 weeks, maximum

4 specialties—sentry, scout or patrol, messenger, or mine dog

15 war dog platoons established, seven in Europe and eight in the Pacific

Standout Canine Soldiers

Sgt. Stubby

Chips

Sgt. Stubby, a pit bull, survived 17 battles during World War I. He was the first dog to be given a rank in the military after he captured a German spy. Stubby also alerted soldiers to gas attacks and survived a grenade attack.

Chips was a German Shepherd mix that served in the 3rd Infantry Division in World War II. Chips attacked enemy gunmen to allow U.S. troops who were trapped on a beach in Italy to escape. For his bravery Chips received the Distinguished Service Cross, Silver Star, and Purple Heart. The awards were later taken back because he wasn't human.

32 breeds initially accepted

7 breeds currently allowed—German Shepherds, Belgian sheepdogs, Doberman pinschers, collies, Siberian huskies, malamutes, and Eskimo dogs

The Army in 1s

To bring to Basic Combat Training (BCT)

1
- pair of white, calf-high, athletic socks
- pair of comfortable shoes
- day's worth of clothes
- combination lock or padlock

100 hours (about four days) of Operation Desert Storm (Persian Gulf War) in January 1991

10 weeks of BCT

$100 Cash in excess of $100 is unauthorized at Ranger School and could get a soldier kicked out.

1,000 approximate number of gallons of fuel a Chinook helicopter holds

100+ miles per hour: speed a Silver Wings parachute jumper reaches during two miles of free fall

$1,000,000 cost of ammunition used in training in 2013

Special Operations Forces

Soldiers in the U.S. Army Special Operations Forces (SOF) are highly trained. The Army SOF includes different groups. Each group performs specialized, dangerous missions.

Army Special Forces: elite soldiers whose missions include special reconnaissance and counterterrorism; commonly referred to as Green Berets

40% of soldiers who are assessed for Army Special Forces are successful and move on to the next phases of training.

5 phases of training

3 words **De Oppresso Liber** meaning "To Liberate the Oppressed," the motto of the Army Special Forces

4 Army Special Forces specialties
- weapons
- engineering
- communications
- medical

1961 first green beret hats are given to the Army Special Forces by President John F. Kennedy

Aviation Regiment (SOAR):

that are usually performed at night. SOAR members are commonly called Night Stalkers.

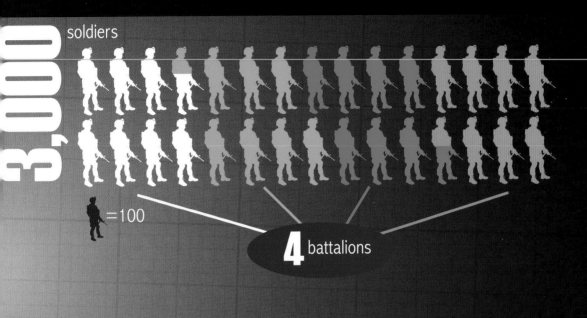

3,000 soldiers

= 100

4 battalions

Rangers:

soldiers who specialize in direct-action raids, such as air assault, facility destruction, and the capture of enemies

52 Military Occupational Specialties (MOS), or jobs, in the 75th Ranger Regiment

8 weeks of training for enlisted soldiers at the Ranger Assessment

5 parts of the Ranger philosophy

1. physical fitness
2. marksmanship

U.S. NAVY

The U.S. Navy can trace its beginnings back to the Revolutionary War (1775–1783). Members of the United States Navy guard their nation's shores and command the seas. The mobility of their fleet of ships allows them be stationed all over the world. Navy sailors stand ready to deal with enemy threats anywhere at any time.

World Class Personnel and Fleet

The unnofficial Naval motto is Latin for "Not self, but country." All current and former Naval sailors have been expected to live by that motto.

Personnel in the U.S. Navy

323,225

Active Duty
201,000
civilian employees

11,087
female officers
(total active and reserve)

Enlisted
264,766

Officers
53,947

4,512
Midshipmen
(sailors in training
to become officers)

Aircraft Carriers:
Rulers of the Sea

Aircraft carriers are one of the most recognizable U.S. Navy ships. These floating military bases station personnel and aircraft throughout the world. They provide bases for aircraft at sea, allowing for quick air strikes from almost anywhere on the planet.

256 ft.: width

The newest class of aircraft carriers is the Gerald R. Ford class. The first ship of this class, the USS *Gerald R. Ford* will be completed in 2015.

Gerald R. Ford Class Stats

3 deck edge elevators

50 years: service life

30+ knots (35 mph): speed

Onboard desalination plants can produce

78 1st Gerald R. Ford class aircraft carrier number

400,000 gallons of fresh water per day.

4 propellers

up to

90 aircraft on the carrier

4,539 crew members

10 of this class of ship planned to be built

800 fewer crew members than the previous CVN 68-class ship

320 feet: the length given for arresting cables to stop planes traveling at 150 mph

1,092 ft: length = 75-story building lying on its side

25 years at sea without refueling

stands as tall as a 24-story building

Aircraft Carrier Strike Group

Aircraft carriers don't travel the open sea alone. They are accompanied by any number of ships, planes, and submarines to keep them safe. Together they are known as an aircraft carrier strike group.

11: number of aircraft carrier strike groups in the Navy as of 2013

100,000: pounds of weaponry carried on an aircraft carrier

CG Ticonderoga class (Cruisers):

guided-missile vessels that support an aircraft carrier

55 feet: width

567 feet: length

330: crew members

22: number in the Navy

DDG Arleigh Burke class (Destroyers):

guided-missile vessels that support an aircraft carrier in battle and in other missions

59 feet: width

505-509 feet: length

276 : crew members

66 : number in the Navy (including those under construction)

Littoral Ships (Independence variant):

built for speed and often used for near-shore missions

103.7 feet: width

419 feet: length

15 to 50 : crew members

4 : number in the Navy

Ballistic Missile Submarines (Ohio class):

provide underwater fire support for the aircraft carrier strike group

42 feet: width

560 feet: length

155 : crew members

18 : number in the Navy (including those under construction)

On Land and at Sea ▫····

width

105 feet
106 feet
105 feet
84 feet
84 feet
84 feet

length

844 feet
802 feet
684 feet
570 feet
609 feet
609 feet

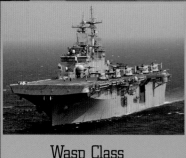

Wasp Class

Tarawa Class

San Antonio Class

Amphibious Assault Ships

can easily maneuver
from sea to land

Amphibious Transport Dock

transport Marines, their
equipment, and supplies

Amphibious vessels serve an important function in the U.S. Navy. They carry equipment, supplies, weapons, and sailors on the open sea. But they can also be used in land battles. The Navy uses different amphibious vessels for different missions.

speed

about 20 knots

about 24 knots

about 22 knots

about 21 knots

about 20 knots

about 20 knots

capacity

1,070 crew

964 crew

800 crew

900 crew

504 crew

504 crew

Austin Class

Harpers Ferry Class

Whidbey Island Class

Dock Landing Ships

transport air cushions for landing craft; provide docking and repair services for small ships, boats, and landing craft

Flying High in the U.S. Navy

While the primary Navy vehicles are ships, aircraft serve important functions in the Navy as well. Aircraft provide protection and warnings to ships and transport personnel and supplies. Aircraft also perform attack missions.

FA/18: used to attack ground targets, enemy ships, or other aircraft

565: FA/18s scheduled for delivery to the U.S. Navy by 2015

60.3 ft.: length

16 ft.: height

44.9 ft.: wingspan

1-2: crew members

flies at **50,000** ft. up to Mach **1.8+**

C-130 Hercules: hauls people and cargo for various missions

97 ft., **9** in.: length

38 ft., **3** in.: height

132 ft., **7** in.: wingspan

5: crew members (also carries 92 troop members)

E-2 Hawkeye: gives information to the carrier strike group, including weather conditions and battle plans

24-ft-wide radar rotodome: This equipment rotates and collects data to warn ships of danger and help in planning attacks. It can track 2,000 targets as far away as 342 miles. It also tracks weather.

360 degrees: radar coverage

5: crew members

57 ft., **6** in.: length

18 ft., **3** in.: height

80 ft., **7** in.: wingspan

Rotary Wing Aircraft (helicopters)

MH-60 Seahawk:

The Seahawk family of helicopters has a combined 2.5 million flight hours in antisubmarine and surface warfare.

64 ft., **10** in.: length

18 ft.: height

3-4: crew members

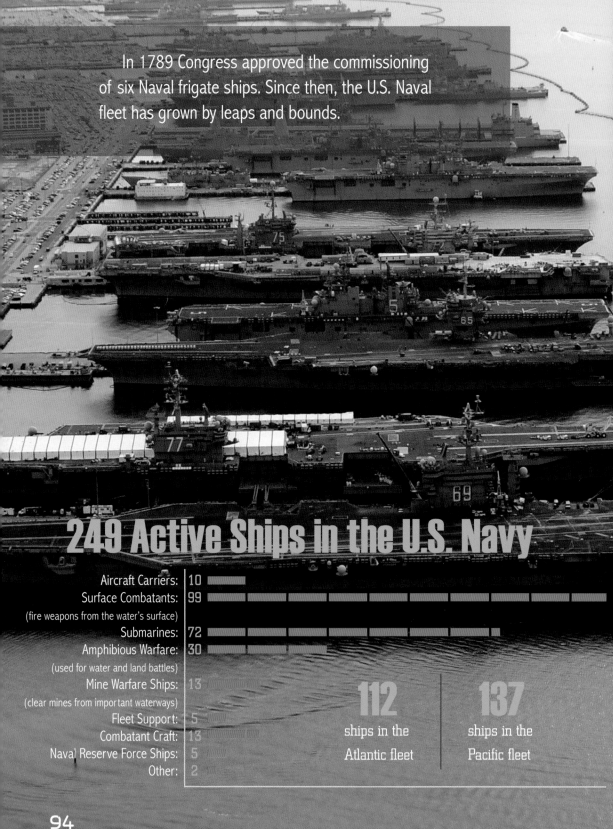

In 1789 Congress approved the commissioning of six Naval frigate ships. Since then, the U.S. Naval fleet has grown by leaps and bounds.

249 Active Ships in the U.S. Navy

Aircraft Carriers:	10	
Surface Combatants:	99	
(fire weapons from the water's surface)		
Submarines:	72	
Amphibious Warfare:	30	
(used for water and land battles)		
Mine Warfare Ships:	13	
(clear mines from important waterways)		
Fleet Support:	5	
Combatant Craft:	13	
Naval Reserve Force Ships:	5	
Other:	2	

112
ships in the
Atlantic fleet

137
ships in the
Pacific fleet

Boot Camp!
Training Sailors

boot camp 8 weeks intense training at the Naval Recruit Training Command at Great Lakes, Illinois

To graduate from boot camp, every recruit must meet these requirements:

run

1.5 miles in:

females: 16:20 minutes

males: 13:40 minutes

SEAL candidates
(Navy special forces): 11 minutes

strength

females: 16 push-ups and
46 sit-ups in 2 minutes

males: 37 push-ups and
46 sit-ups in 2 minutes

SEAL candidates: 42 push-ups and
50 sit-ups in 2 minutes and do
6 pull-ups

fire

an M9 Beretta pistol
and M-870 shotgun

jump

off a 10-foot tower
into water below

swim

50 yards and spend
5 minutes in the
prone position
(dead man's float)

Battle Stations (Final Test)

- 12 hours: length of time final test lasts
  - involves 17 shipboard scenarios that a sailor could encounter onboard a ship
  - Successful completion of Battle Stations is required for boot camp graduation.

Becoming a SEAL
SEa – Air – Land

The Navy SEALs are an elite fighting force that are part of the U.S. military's special operations forces. They are sent on some of the most dangerous missions imaginable. To become a Navy SEAL, a man must first join the Navy. Then he must pass the SEAL physical screening test. Finally, he has to complete highly advanced training, including Basic Underwater Demolition (BUDs) training, jump school, and SEAL Qualification Training (SQT).

Training includes:

running 200 miles

3 weeks of combat swimmer training

running **13** miles wearing 65 pounds of gear

26 weeks of SQT

5 days in a simulation as a captured POW

parachuting from 36,000 feet in jump school

28 days of cold weather mountaineering training

Every Year: About 2,500 Navy SEALs serve in the United States. On any day they can be deployed to 30 countries.

1,000

men start SEAL training every year

only 25% of the men complete the training

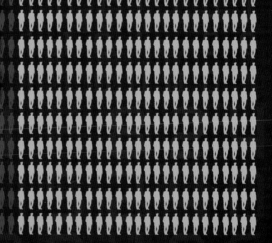

Upon completion of training, SEALs get a **$15,000** bonus.

• Only men are allowed to become Navy SEALs. This rule may change. The ban on women in combat roles was lifted in 2013.

Life at Sea

Men and women in the U.S. Navy spend a large part of their time at sea. But sailors have very different experiences depending upon what type of vessel they sail on. Here's how life on board an aircraft carrier and a submarine compares.

Deployment

A submarine can be at sea up to 80 days before resurfacing.

Sailors on an aircraft carrier can be out to sea up to 9 months.

Workdays

Days on a submarine are 18 hours long instead of 24 hours. Crews work in rotating shifts:

6 hours on and 12 hours off

Depending on a sailor's job, he or she may work up to 22 hours in a day on an aircraft carrier.

Clothes

Sub crew members wear 1-piece blue overalls and sneakers. The overalls reduce the amount of clothing necessary on subs.

On an aircraft carrier flight deck, crews wear different colored shirts depending on their jobs.

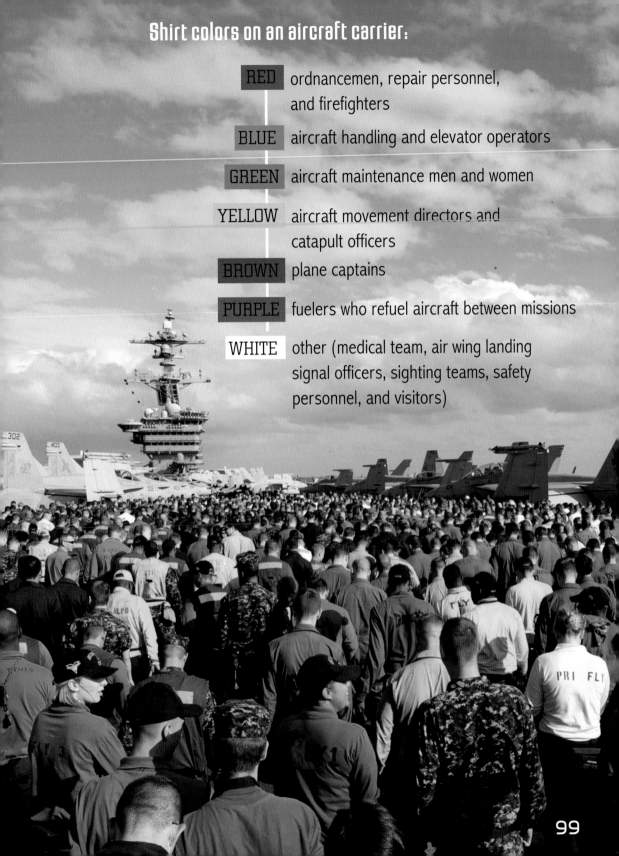

Shirt colors on an aircraft carrier:

RED ordnancemen, repair personnel, and firefighters

BLUE aircraft handling and elevator operators

GREEN aircraft maintenance men and women

YELLOW aircraft movement directors and catapult officers

BROWN plane captains

PURPLE fuelers who refuel aircraft between missions

WHITE other (medical team, air wing landing signal officers, sighting teams, safety personnel, and visitors)

Into the Deep: Submarines

Hidden beneath ocean waves, submarines have always had an advantage over surface ships. Subs have improved dramatically since the first one was built. The first sub was called the Turtle Sub.

Turtle Sub

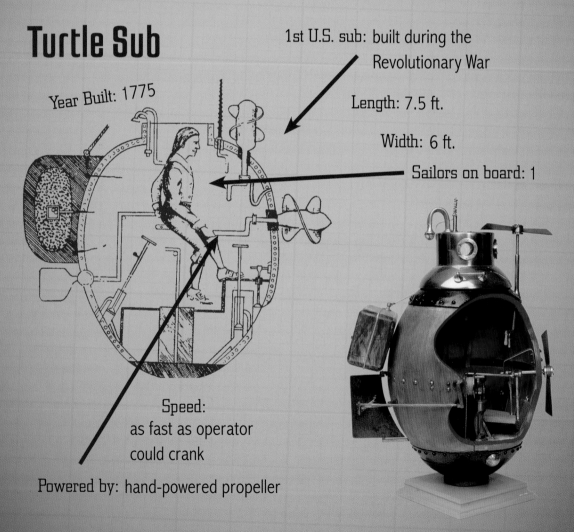

Year Built: 1775

1st U.S. sub: built during the Revolutionary War

Length: 7.5 ft.

Width: 6 ft.

Sailors on board: 1

Speed: as fast as operator could crank

Powered by: hand-powered propeller

Weaponry: 1 mine torpedo loaded with 150 pounds of gunpowder

Fleet Ballistic Missile Subs, Ohio Class:

(also called "Boomers")
largest nuclear sub

- Year built: 1981 to present

- Powered by: nuclear power

- Length: 560 ft. (nearly as long as 2 football fields)

- Width: 30 ft. (3-story building)

- Weaponry: ballistic missiles and MK-48 torpedoes

- Sailors on board: 15 officers
  140 enlisted sailors

Naval Weapons

Navy vessels require large, powerful weapons. The Tomahawk Cruise Missile and the MK-48 Heavyweight Torpedo are two long-range weapons.

Tomahawk Cruise Missile:

This long-range cruise missile can be launched from surface ships and submarines. It can carry one large warhead or a canister of small bombs. It is highly accurate and is mainly used for land attacks.

Length: 20 ft., 6 in.

Diameter: 20.4 in.

Wingspan: 8 ft., 9 in.

Weight: 2,900 lb.

Range: 1,554 miles

Speed: about 550 mph

First operational use: Operation Desert Storm, 1991

MK-48 Heavyweight Torpedo:

This torpedo is only used by submarines. It is a self-propelled, guided projectile that operates underwater. It is designed to set off an explosion either on contact with a target or near a target. It carries 650 pounds of high explosives and can sink subs and large ships.

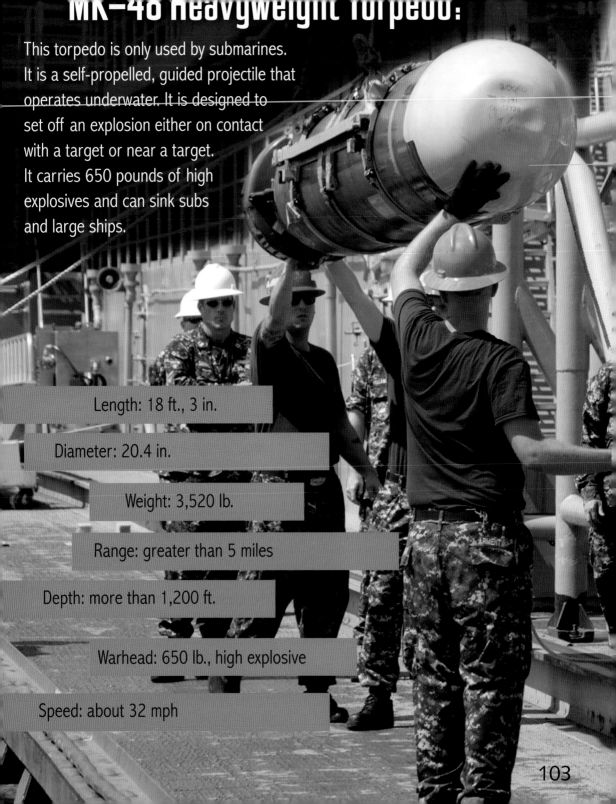

Length: 18 ft., 3 in.

Diameter: 20.4 in.

Weight: 3,520 lb.

Range: greater than 5 miles

Depth: more than 1,200 ft.

Warhead: 650 lb., high explosive

Speed: about 32 mph

Counting by

11

There are 11 fleet bands in the U.S. Navy. They are made up of professional musicians from around the country. They play in concerts, march in parades, and perform for leaders.

22

On December 22, 1775, the Continental Congress created the Continental Navy.

33

Code 33 is the department in the U.S. Navy that is responsible for developing warfare and energy technologies.

44

VA-44 Hornets operated as attackers and fighters during the Korean War.

55

Fifty-five women graduated from the U.S. Naval Academy in 1980, the first graduating class to include females.

66

During recruit training, a Navy SEAL can be away from home for up to 66 weeks.

77

The CVN 77 aircraft carrier was named after George H.W. Bush. He was the Navy's youngest World War II pilot and the 41st president of the United States.

88

From 2001 to 2008, the Navy sponsored car number 88 in NASCAR's Nationwide series.

99

In 2009 the U.S. Navy saved $99 million dollars in fuel by decreasing how much energy each ship used.

Attack on Pearl Harbor

On December 7, 1941, Japan pulled the United States into World War II. The Japanese did this with a surprise attack on the U.S. Navy base at Pearl Harbor, Hawaii. They hoped to damage the U.S. Navy so badly that it couldn't fight back.

6:45 a.m. A U.S. ship spots a small Japanese submarine trying to enter Pearl Harbor. The ship fires on the sub and sinks it. U.S. forces do not realize this is part of a larger attack.

7:02 a.m. An Army radar station near Pearl Harbor gets a signal that a large group of planes is approaching. Radar technology is new, and technicians don't realize that the planes are Japanese.

7:55 a.m. The Japanese planes begin dropping bombs on Pearl Harbor and the surrounding areas.

8:10 a.m. A bomb blasts through the deck of the USS *Arizona*. It sets off more than 1 million pounds of gunpowder. The resulting explosion kills 1,177 men.

8:54 a.m. A second wave of Japanese planes joins the attack. This time U.S. troops are more prepared to fight back with anti-aircraft fire.

9:30 a.m. A bomb hits the USS *Shaw* and blows off the front end of the ship.

10:00 a.m. The attack ends.

United States | Japan

Ships sunk, beached, or damaged	Aircraft destroyed or damaged	Personnel wounded	Personnel killed
21 / at least 1	323 / 103	1,178 / unknown	2,378 / 64

Midway: A Decisive Battle

The World War II Battle of Midway is one of the most important battles in U.S. Navy history. The United States had three aircraft carriers based around the Pacific islands of Midway. The Japanese hoped to destroy those carriers. But U.S. dive bombers caught Japanese carriers refueling and rearming their planes. They attacked. Japanese losses were huge. This defeat of the Japanese eventually led to the Allied victory in World War II.

6 number of months after the attack on Pearl Harbor that the Battle of Midway took place

4 number of days the sea and air battle lasted—from June 4–7th, 1942

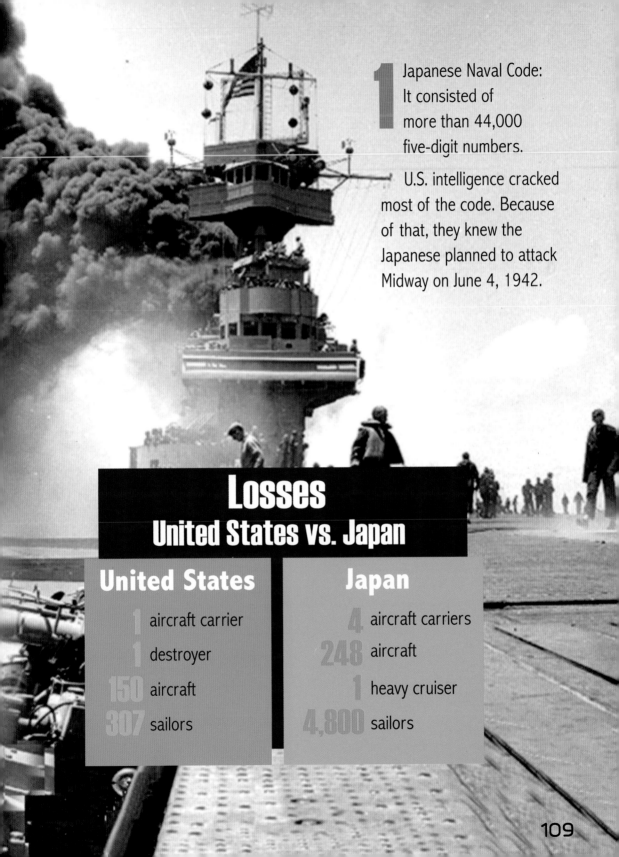

1 Japanese Naval Code: It consisted of more than 44,000 five-digit numbers.

U.S. intelligence cracked most of the code. Because of that, they knew the Japanese planned to attack Midway on June 4, 1942.

Losses
United States vs. Japan

United States		Japan	
1	aircraft carrier	4	aircraft carriers
1	destroyer	248	aircraft
150	aircraft	1	heavy cruiser
307	sailors	4,800	sailors

Index

Published by Capstone Press,
1710 Roe Crest Drive, North Mankato, Minnesota 56003
www.capstoneyoungreaders.com

Library of Congress Cataloging-in-Publication Data
Cataloging-in-publication information is on file with the Library of Congress.
ISBN 978-1-62370-061-4
ISBN 978-1-62370-188-8

Photo Credits
Alamy: DIZ Muenchen GmbH, Sueddeutsche Zeitung Photo, 45, Lightroom Photos, 68-69, LM, 47 (top); AP Photo: Joe Rosenthal, 14-15; Corbis, 44, 104 (middle top), 105 (77), Aero Graphics, Inc, 36 (bottom), Bettmann, 12b, 13b, 33 (top right), 46b, 47 (middle), Peter Turnley, 31 (bottom right); DoD photo by Cpl. Tommy Huynh, USMC, 4-5 (background), Sgt. Brian Erickson, USA, 58, Spc. De'Yonte Mosley, USA, 75t, SSgt. Jeff Kaus, USMC, 5b; Getty Images: Archive Photos/ MPI, 100 (left), Bert Hardy, 13t, Buyenlarge, 12 (inset), Photoquest, 47b, Robert Nickelsberg, 73t, Science & Society Picture Library, 100 (right), Time Life Pictures/David Scherman, 70; iStockphotos: Frank Ramspott, 56 (map), Library of Congress, 33 (top left), 61, New York World-Telegram & Sun Newspaper Photograph Collection, 4; Naval History & Heritage Command, 15 (map), 106-107; Shutterstock: arindambanerjee, 28, Konstantnin, 22t, Vartanov Anatoly, 23m, 62 (M9); SuperStock: ClassicStock.com, 104 (right middle), 105 (22), U.S. Air Force photo, 37b, 42b, 46t, 56 (inset), 57, A1C Benjamin Wiseman, 36t, MSgt. Lance Cheung, 37t, MSgt. Russell E. Cooley IV, 40-41, MSgt. Stan Parker, 38-39, MSgt. William Greer, 50, Sarah M. Corrice, 54-55, SrA Brett Clashman, 33 (bottom left), SrA Christopher Griffin, 34-35, Sgt. Kimberly Lamb, 62 (MK19-3), SSgt. Aaron D. Allmon II, 62 (M120), SSgt. Angelita M. Lawrence, 80-81, SSgt. Ashley Hawkins, 32, SSgt. Christopher Hubenthal, 37m, SSgt. M. Erick Reynolds, 43t, SSgt. Michael B. Keller, 33 (background), TSgt Michael Haggerty, 33 (bottom right), TSgt. Francisco V. Govea II, 78m, TSgt. Justin D. Pyle, 42t, TSgt. Sean M. Worrell, 71, TSgt. Kit Thompson, 48-49, U.S. Army photo, cover, 43b, 46m, 60, 73b, 74l, 78b, 79b, Sgt. Heather Denby, 79t, Sgt. Igor Paustovski, 72, Sgt. John Crosby, 62-63 (background), Sgt. Kissta DiGregorio, 75m, SGM. Rich Greene, 75 (bottom left), Spc. Gregory Gieske, 62 (M109A6), SSgt. James Allen, 75 (bottom right), SSgt. Jason Epperson, 66-67, SSgt. Kevin L. Moses Sr, 74r; U.S. Army Signal Corps photo, 5 (top left); U.S. Coast Guard photo by CPHOM Robert F. Sargent, 76-77; U.S. Marine Corps photo, 62 (M224), Cpl. Benjamin R. Reynolds, 24t, Cpl. Dwight A. Henderson, 10-11, Cpl. Eric Quintanillla, 16 (top right), Cpl. Liz Gleason, 21 (top left), Cpl. Marionne T. Mangrum, 31 (bottom right), Cpl. Michael Augusto, 25b, Cpl. Michael S. Cifuentes, 18, , 25t, Cpl. Richard Blumenstein, 30-31, Cpl. Walter D. Marino II, 16 (top left), , 21 (top right), GySgt. Kevin W. Williams, 24b, GySgt. Scott Dunn, 24m, LCpl. Angela Hitchcock, 64-65, LCpl. Bridget M. Keane, 21 (bottom both), LCpl. Crystal Druery, 16 (bottom right), LCpl. Jacob W. Chase, 23t, LCpl. Jhonson Simeon, 29t, LCpl. Kyle McNally, 31 (top right), LCpl. Matthew J. Anderson, 6, LCpl. Matthew Manning, 29b, LCpl. Michael Ito, 16 (bottom left), LCpl. Pedro Cardenas, 20b, LCpl. Scott W. Whiting, 8b, Pfc. Crystal Druery, 20t, Pfc. Dalton Precht, 23b, Pfc. Kasey Peacock, 22m, Sgt. Jose Nava, 16 (background), SSgt. Danielle M. Bacon, 31 (top left); U.S. Navy graphic, 86-87, U.S. Navy photo, 104 (left middle), , 105 (44), Lt. Liza Swart, 95, MC1 Cassandra Thompson, 89m, MC1 Curtis K. Biasi, 104 (right top), MC1 Curtis K. Biasi, 105 (88), MC1 James Kimber, 89b, MC1 James Kimber, 101, MC1 Ricardo Danan, 103, MC1 Thomas Coffman, 78t, MC1 Tommy Lamkin, 88, MC1 Woody Paschall, 102, MC2 Daniel Barker, 104 (left top), MC2 Daniel Barker, 105 (11), MC2 Dominique Pineiro, 105b, MC2 Ernest R. Scott, 94, MC2 James R. Evans, 93 (both), MC2 James R. Evans, 99, MC2 Jason R. Zalasky, 90 (middle and right) MC2 Jon Dasbach, 89t, MC2 Kevin S. O'Brien, 104 (middle middle), MC2 Kevin S. O'Brien, 105 (55), MC2 Marcos T. Hernandez, 104 (right bottom), MC2 Marcos T. Hernandez, 105 (66), MC2 Matthew R. White, 91m, MC2 Zachary L. Borden, 90l, MC3 Jonathan Sunderman, 26-27, MC3 Jonathan Sunderman, 91r, MC3 Kenneth Abbate, 5 (top right), MC3 Mikey Mulcare, 84, MCSA Daniel J. Walls, 7, MCSN Jared M. King, 92t, MCSN John Grandin, 91l, MCSN Sabrina Fine, 98ri, PH2 Mark A. Ebert, 92b, PHC John E. Gay, 98l, SN Trevor Welsh, 8t; U.S. Navy SEAL and SWCC photo, 104 (left bottom and middle bottom), 105 (33), Wikimedia: US Navy/PH2 William G. Roy/post-work Cobatfor, 108-109; Wikipedia: PEOSoldier, 22b, 62 (M24A3)

Design Elements
Shutterstock: aarrows, Akai37, Aleksandar Mijatovic, Bojanovic, Darq, Filip Bjorkman, kednert, MIRJANA BANJAC, Oleg Zabielin, Paul Stringer, URRRA, Yaraz, zsooofija,

Editorial Credits
Mandy Robbins and Brenda Haugen, editors; Heidi Thompson, designer; Charmaine Whitman, production specialist

Printed in China   012014   007988